GIRLS' HEALTH ™

EATING DISORDERS

TAMMY LASER AND STEPHANIE WATSON

rosen publishing's
rosen
central

WITHDRAWN

NEW YORK

Published in 2012 by The Rosen Publishing Group, Inc.

29 East 21st Street, New York, NY 10010
Copyright © 2012 by The Rosen Publishing Group, Inc.

First Edition

Library of Congress Cataloging-in-Publication Data

Laser, Tammy.
Eating Disorders/Tammy Laser, Stephanie Watson.— 1st ed.
     p. cm.—(Girls' health)
Includes bibliographical references and index.
ISBN 978-1-4488-4573-6 (lib. bdg.)
1. Eating disorders—Juvenile literature. I. Watson, Stephanie, 1969– II. Title.
RC552.E18L37 2012
616.85'26—dc22

                                                                2011008898

Manufactured in the United States of America

CPSIA Compliance Information: Batch #S11YA: For further information, contact Rosen Publishing, New York, New York, at 1-800-237-9932.

CONTENTS

INTRODUCTION

You've likely heard someone say, "She is so skinny! She must be anorexic," when referring to someone on TV or in a movie or even in the halls at school. Or maybe someone has said that about you. But eating disorders, such as anorexia, are more complicated than that. You can rarely look at someone and determine if he or she is suffering from an eating disorder. For one thing, there are several different types of eating disorders, and not all of them result in extreme weight loss. They can affect men or women of any age. And eating disorders are mental conditions as well as physical. You cannot simply look at a person and see that he or she is suffering from a mental condition. That determination is made by a mental health professional or doctor.

In this book, we will take a look at the different types of eating disorders, how they affect those suffering from them, what causes eating disorders, and how a person can find his or her way down the road to recovery. Once you are able to understand the realities of eating disorders, you can better determine how to help yourself or someone you know who may be suffering. And the next time you hear someone say, "She must be anorexic," you can be more prepared to shed some light on the reality of that condition. And if you are personally suffering from an eating disorder, you can learn more about your disease and where to go for help.

Eating disorders can involve eating too much or too little, or eating followed by purging. But one thing that all of them have in common is that the sufferer has an unhealthy relationship with food.

CHAPTER one

WHAT ARE EATING DISORDERS?

The National Eating Disorders Association estimates that five to ten million girls and young women, and another one million boys and men, have some form of an eating disorder. As many as 15 percent of young women have unhealthy attitudes toward food and their bodies, according to a report by GirlPower.gov, a Web site sponsored by the U.S. Department of Health and Human Services.

Worse, an estimated one thousand young women die each year from anorexia nervosa as a result of starvation, permanent damage to their vital organs, or suicide. Twelve times as many girls and women die from anorexia than from all other causes of death for that age group, according to the National Institute of Mental Health. Eating disorders can be cured if they are diagnosed early enough. The recovery process can be extremely difficult, as it is very long and involves professional therapy, medication (for some), and deep inner work.

WHAT DEFINES AN EATING DISORDER?

Eating disorders are classified as psychiatric illnesses because they arise from an unhealthy relationship with food. Eating can cause

Many people closely monitor their weight, but for a teen suffering from an eating disorder, weight becomes an obsession. Even when she is at her healthiest weight, a teen may see herself as overweight.

discomfort, guilt, discord with others, or self-hatred. Eating disorders derive from numerous influences, including low self-esteem, abuse in the home, or peer pressure. Any or all of these can make food one way that people can control something in their life. Or food can become a symbol of something bad that might be occurring in someone's life. The negative feelings about food can become overpowering—so much so that they can interfere with a person's health. Eating becomes disordered and can cause emotional and physical problems.

The fact that eating disorders are considered psychiatric illnesses does not mean that eating disorders are psychosomatic. A psychosomatic disease is one that a person imagines, but does not actually have. Eating disorders are very real, even though part of the eating disorder is caused by a distorted self-image. And the end result of untreated eating disorders is just as serious and potentially fatal as a physical disease that is left untreated.

Eating disorders often overlap in one person. For example, an anorexic person may use bulimic behaviors as a way of further reducing his or her weight. That person may also begin exercising excessively. Add the overuse of harsh laxatives and diuretics, and you've created a complex behavioral pattern (which can include mental, emotional, and spiritual patterns) that can take months or even years to overcome.

WHAT IS ANOREXIA NERVOSA?

Anorexia nervosa is an eating disorder in which a person is preoccupied with food, dieting, and thinness to the point of starvation. People with anorexia eat very little or refuse to eat at all. A person is diagnosed with anorexia nervosa if she weighs 15 percent less than the expected body weight for her age, height, and physical build, if she hasn't had a menstrual cycle in three consecutive months, and if she exhibits extreme concern with "being fat."

A teen suffering from compulsive exercise disorder does not stop exercising when he or she is tired. Exercise and weight loss become an obsession.

WHAT IS BULIMIA NERVOSA?

People with bulimia may eat what seems like a normal amount of food or may even overeat. But then they find a way to purge, or rid themselves of the food they have taken in. Purging can be done by inducing vomiting, using laxatives (which cause a bowel movement), using diuretics (which cause frequent urination), or exercising.

As bulimia progresses, what started as a once-in-a-while behavior becomes a daily routine. The person may induce vomiting one or more times each day. Someone who is bulimic may be of normal weight, but fasting and purging take a serious toll on the body.

WHAT IS BINGE EATING DISORDER?

Binge eaters have uncontrolled bouts of eating, but they don't purge after eating. A binge eater may eat secretly and will not stop when he or she is full.

Between 10 and 15 percent of people who are mildly obese and who are trying to lose weight may be binge eaters, according to the National Institutes of Health (NIH). Depression, feelings of helplessness, and other psychological problems often trigger binge eating.

WHAT IS COMPULSIVE EXERCISE DISORDER?

Some people seem to get caught up in a vicious cycle of burning calories, trying to control their weight.

Compulsive exercisers may spend several hours every day working out. Their goal is not to stay fit, but to gain more control over their lives. Compulsive exercise disorder (also called exercise addiction) often goes along with compulsive overeating, but it has been noted in people with anorexia and bulimia as well.

AND
FACTS

MYTH **You can tell whether someone has an eating disorder by how skinny the person is.**

FACT Many people with anorexia, bulimia, and other eating disorders are of average weight or just a few pounds underweight, so their weight loss isn't noticeable. Many thin people are naturally that way because of genetics or a high metabolism.

MYTH **You can't die from an eating disorder.**

FACT Disordered eating can deprive your body of the vitamins and other nutrients it needs to survive. If these levels become too low, you can get very sick. And if you develop low potassium or an electrolyte imbalance, your heart can stop beating and you'll die.

MYTH **You have to be thin to be happy.**

FACT Your body size shouldn't have anything to do with how good you feel about yourself. You should see yourself as a beautiful, important person, regardless of what clothing size you wear.

CHAPTER two

EDUCATING YOURSELF ON EATING DISORDERS

Eating disorders can take over your life. Unless you get help—and want help—you may become very ill and you may die. Each of the following disorders is a different type of behavior, but many people with eating disorders suffer from symptoms that are related to more than one condition. You need to understand what the different eating disorders are and how they can hurt you in order to get help for your problem.

THE STRUGGLE WITH ANOREXIA NERVOSA

An estimated 1 to 2 percent of women have struggled with anorexia at some point in their lives, according to the NIH. The word "anorexia" means "loss of appetite." People who have this disorder become so obsessed with losing weight that they ignore their body's hunger signals and literally starve themselves. Denying their hunger helps people with anorexia feel more in control. But this disorder can be very dangerous. Losing too much weight can cause serious health problems and even death.

Isabelle Caro was the face of the "No Anorexia" ad campaign, a controversial campaign that showed the unhealthy form of a person suffering from anorexia. Caro passed away in November 2010 from her illness.

LEARNING ABOUT ANOREXIA

There are two types of anorexia. People with anorexia either diet and/ or exercise constantly to keep their weight down, or they eat a lot of food at once (called bingeing) and then get rid of it (purging) to avoid gaining weight. Some of the warning signs of anorexia nervosa include the following:

- Being very afraid of gaining weight, even if you aren't overweight. If you obsess about every bite of food that you put in your mouth, worrying that it has too many calories, you may

have anorexia. That fear can begin to control you to the point where you think about avoiding food all the time.
- Not liking what you see in the mirror. Even though everyone tells you you're thin, you see a fat person staring back at you.
- Using laxatives, enemas (liquid placed in the rectum to have a bowel movement), or diuretics to help you lose weight. Or you may cut back severely on the amount of food you eat, or you may exercise too much.

ANOREXIA'S EFFECTS

Anorexia can lead to these effects on your body:

- Weight loss
- Feeling cold all the time
- Lanugo—a fine hair that grows all over your body
- Disruption or loss of monthly menstruation (your period)
- Feeling tired and/or weak
- Fainting
- Headaches
- Pasty complexion
- Yellow palms and soles of your feet (due to nutrient imbalance)
- Heart problems
- Infertility (the inability to have children)

THE STRUGGLE WITH BULIMIA NERVOSA

Although bulimia nervosa has been known since the 1950s, it wasn't well understood until the 1980s. Celebrities such as Paula Abdul, a judge on the television series *Live to Dance*, and Geri Halliwell, formerly of the band the Spice Girls, have brought this disorder to the public's attention.

LEARNING ABOUT BULIMIA

Bulimia involves cycles of bingeing—as many as five thousand calories or more at once—and then purging the food by vomiting or using drugs such as laxatives or diuretics. People with bulimia may purge once or several times a day. Bingeing and purging can have devastating effects on the body.

People who have bulimia may be hard to spot because their weight may not be much higher or lower than average. The most obvious sign that people have bulimia is that they disappear after meals, usually going into the bathroom. You may see them purge by strict dieting, fasting, vigorous exercise, vomiting, or using laxatives and diuretics. They are preoccupied with body weight, constantly getting on the scale.

BULIMIA'S EFFECTS

These are some of the physical side effects of bulimia:

- Frequent complaints about feeling dizzy, light-headed, or faint
- Bruised or callused knuckles and fingers from sticking fingers down the throat to induce vomiting
- Swollen cheeks, giving the face a puffy look
- Sore throat, sore and swollen glands in the neck
- Dry skin, brittle hair, and obvious hair loss
- Fine hair called lanugo growing on the face, back, and arms
- Dental problems, including tooth and gum decay
- Heartburn and bloating
- Frequent headaches and complaints of being cold
- Tingling in the hands, feet, and face and irregular or slow heart-beat caused by low potassium or other vitamin deficiencies

- Depression and/or sudden mood swings
- Long-term effects may include loss of tooth enamel, arthritis, osteoporosis (a disease that causes bones to weaken and break), back and joint pain, poor circulation, heart problems, sleep problems, and fatigue

THE STRUGGLE WITH BINGE EATING DISORDER

Everyone overeats occasionally. Around the holidays or on vacation, when there are so many good things to eat, you know how easy it is to eat too much. You wind up with a stomachache and an urge to take a long nap.

A person suffering from binge eating disorder can sometimes no longer recognize the feeling of being full and will continue to eat, knowing that what she is doing is unhealthy.

That kind of bingeing isn't harmful if it doesn't become a habit. When someone binge eats regularly, that person's weight can balloon to a very unhealthy level. And when a person has eaten sparingly for a long time and then eats a huge amount of food in a short period of time, a binge can be fatal.

LEARNING ABOUT BINGE EATING DISORDER

For people who are binge eaters, the urge to binge becomes constant and powerful. There is an anxiety beneath the compulsion to eat in such an unhealthy manner and an inability to stop eating. These are the trouble signs of binge eating disorder to watch for:

- Episodes of binge eating. Even though binge eaters tend to binge in secret, it's possible you might see them eating more at one time than appears to be healthy.
- Eating when not hungry. Binge eaters eat at any time, day or night, sometimes soon after a heavy meal. They have trouble identifying real hunger and fullness and feel hungry all the time. The need to continue eating has little to do with hunger. Instead, they are trying to feed, or soothe, a different kind of need.
- Grazing. Eating often throughout the day, often in front of other people.
- Frequent dieting. Oddly, binge eaters and compulsive overeaters are often on diets, at least publicly. They may talk about food a lot and spend time working on menus.
- Feeling unable to stop eating voluntarily. At a point when most people would be full, binge overeaters continue to eat, consuming huge amounts of food.
- Awareness that their eating patterns are abnormal. Binge eaters will admit to eating too much at a time, but they may also tell you that they just can't help themselves.

- Constant weight changes. Binge eaters lose and gain weight constantly. This pattern is sometimes called yo-yo dieting. Usually, binge eaters can diet successfully for a short period of time and lose weight. Then they suddenly gain back the weight, and usually more.
- Depression. Binge eaters get depressed because they never feel as though they can control events in their lives.
- Relating their self-esteem and success to their weight. Binge eaters define how "good" or "bad" they are based on what foods they eat and how much they weigh. They may constantly put themselves down, saying cruel things about how they eat and look.

THE EFFECTS OF BINGE EATING

The body's reaction to continual overeating is the opposite of what happens in anorexic or bulimic eating disorders. There are many changes to the body that take place when a person constantly overeats. These are a few of those changes:

- Weight gain
- Feeling warm or hot much of the time
- Fast or irregular heart rate, high blood pressure, hormone imbalances, and possibly raised cholesterol levels. These conditions are common in overweight people and could lead to serious heart disease.
- Joint pain, breathing difficulty, and poor circulation caused by the additional stress placed on the body by excess weight
- Stomach and intestinal problems
- Exhaustion, weakness, and dizziness. These are brought on by stress, nutritional imbalances, fast heart rate, and high blood pressure. Excess weight and increased digestive activity

from eating too much places greater pressure on the binge eater's body.

THE STRUGGLE WITH COMPULSIVE EXERCISE DISORDER

You've been told all your life that exercise is good for you. And that's true, up to a point. But there is a point at which exercise stops being beneficial and becomes a psychological disorder called compulsive exercise disorder or exercise addiction.

LEARNING ABOUT COMPULSIVE EXERCISE DISORDER

You probably know at least one dedicated athlete—a person who exercises regularly and stays in good shape through weight training or aerobic sessions. Maybe you are that type of exerciser yourself. That is a healthy way to stay in shape.

Compulsive exercisers go beyond regular workouts. They exercise to or even past the point of pain to burn calories and lose weight. Their self-esteem is directly related to how much they have exercised in a given day, and if they are unable to exercise as much as they believe they should, they become depressed. Compulsive exercise is one of the symptoms of anorexia and bulimia, but it can also occur as a separate disorder. What happens to the person who gets caught up in its unhealthy cycle is similar to what happens to people with other eating disorders.

There are two main reasons why compulsive exercisers do what they do. First, they feel—consciously or not—an enormous need to control a lifestyle or situation that they believe is out of control. It doesn't matter what or where the trouble is—at school, at home with parents or siblings, at work, or in friendships or romantic relationships. The second reason is to lose weight and maintain what may be an unrealistic body image. Compulsive exercisers believe that the more they work out, the thinner they will become. Unfortunately, that isn't always true. Too frequently, compulsive exercise is teamed with compulsive overeating. The person gets so hungry from all the exercise and stringent dieting that he or she binge eats and gains back the weight.

Here are some of the warning signs of compulsive exercise:

- Exercising daily for hours at a time, either in a gym or at home
- Forcing yourself to exercise, even if you don't feel well, or even if you have an injury

Some of the signs of compulsive exercise disorder are isolation, constant worry about weight control, hiding the amount of time spent exercising, or disinterest in things that don't involve exercise.

- Exercising instead of participating in social activities, work, or school
- Constantly talking or worrying about dieting, exercise, and weight control
- Spending long periods of time alone. Compulsive exercisers become skilled at hiding the amount of exercise they do from family or friends.
- Showing signs of eating disorders. Compulsive exercise often develops along with anorexia or bulimia.

THE EFFECTS OF COMPULSIVE EXERCISE DISORDER

People who have anorexia and bulimia in addition to compulsive exercise disorder don't eat enough to compensate for the amount of exercise they do. This puts a lot of strain on their bodies. The combination of not eating enough and exercising too much over a long period of time can permanently damage internal organs and bone structure. Eventually, if you're combining starvation and exercise, you could die.

If you're exercising too often, especially if you're not eating enough, you could see any of these effects on your body:

- Dehydration, if you're not getting enough fluids
- Fatigue, insomnia, and depression
- Injuries to the joints, bones, muscles, and cartilage
- Loss of menstruation

These eating disorders are very dangerous and can cause permanent physical and emotional damage if they are not diagnosed and treated. If you think you might have one or more of these disorders, or if you suspect that a family member or friend may have an eating disorder, find help as quickly as possible. Remember that you are not alone. You can talk to someone you trust, such as a friend, a teacher, a coach, your parents, a sibling, a guidance counselor, or your doctor.

10 GREAT
QUESTIONS
When You're Asking for Help

1 Do I have an eating disorder, and what do you think caused it?

2 How has my eating disorder affected my body?

3 Am I over/underweight?

4 Will I have to have tests to check my health and, if so, which tests will I have?

5 What treatments do you recommend to help me get well?

6 How can I control my urge to overeat, binge and purge, or not eat?

7 How can I get on a healthy diet and stick to it?

8 What kinds of exercise should I be doing?

9 How can I deal with my negative self-image?

10 How can I cope with the other emotional issues that led to my eating disorder?

CHAPTER three

CAUSES OF EATING DISORDERS

Medical professionals have learned a great deal about the symptoms and side effects of eating disorders in the past twenty years, but they still don't understand why one person develops an eating disorder while another person with the same background does not. The true cause of eating disorders—if there is a single cause—has yet to be discovered.

It would be easy to believe that eating disorders are all about food, but that isn't the case. Eating behavior is only one part of a complex mystery. The way people with eating disorders eat—or don't eat—is the outward symptom of their inner problems and turmoil.

Despite differences in the way people develop and experience eating disorders, these people do have certain things in common. The need to be perfect, the need to meet unreasonably high expectations, and the need to feel in control of at least one aspect of their lives are some of the forces that drive the development of eating disorders.

WHAT ARE THE OUTSIDE INFLUENCES?

You may feel a lot of pressure to be thin and do well in everything you try, from school to sports. Especially if you're already

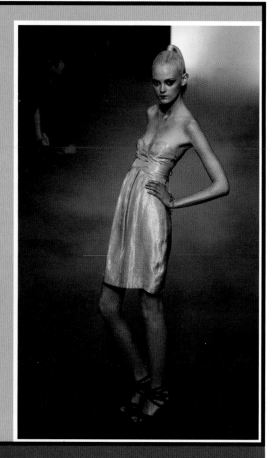

Many experts blame the fashion industry for perpetuating thinness as the ideal, which may lead to the development of eating disorders in young people.

struggling with internal anxieties and self-doubt, these outside pressures can make you even more vulnerable to developing an eating disorder.

THE EFFECTS OF SOCIETY

Our society has an unhealthy pre-occupation with weight and body image, placing a high value on thinness. In fact, many people believe that in order to be beautiful, you have to be thin.

Television, movies, and magazines all promote this unnatural image. The models are rail thin with not an ounce of fat or a smudge of cellulite on their bodies. Seeing these images constantly can make you believe that everyone should look this way. It can make you have negative feelings about yourself because you don't look this way. In fact, very few people in the world are as thin as models. That type of body is almost impossible to achieve.

Some people become anorexic or bulimic because they believe being skinny is the only way they will be accepted or loved. They literally starve themselves nearly to death trying to meet someone else's unrealistic expectations for body size and shape.

THE INFLUENCE OF FAMILY AND FRIENDS

You draw important information about who you are and how you should behave through contact with other people. This information comes first, and perhaps most powerfully, from your parents. Your parents may take more control over your life than is necessary or healthy. Young people who have anorexia, for example, are usually the children of controlling parents. They are obedient children and are not likely to rebel. Other parents may not take any control over your life, leaving you to grow up without any support. Some parents may be emotionally, sexually, or physically abusive. In all these cases, you do not experience a healthy and functional family life and you might turn to food to manage the dysfunction.

You draw other cues about yourself from siblings, friends, teachers, coaches, guidance counselors, and others who become important in your life. If you try to fit into a clique at school or match the academic or athletic achievements of a popular person at school and fail, you may become depressed, and that can pave the way for an eating disorder. If your brother or sister is great at sports or does well in school, he or she may be held up to you as an example. This not only lowers your self-esteem, it also sets up a rivalry in which you may believe you're doomed to failure because you do not think that you are as talented as your sibling.

The influence that key people in your life have on you can be positive or negative. The influence that a strong, positive role model might have on you could turn out to be two-sided. Following the lead of an inspirational or extremely talented person could make you more ambitious and improve your abilities. On the other hand, trying to live up to someone's high-achieving example and falling short could badly damage an already fragile self-image.

In the same way, negative influences can cut both ways. You might look at someone whom you feel is a poor role model and decide not to be like that person. Or you might think that person is having more fun than you are and you may copy him or her. Some people get involved in drug abuse and criminal behavior because they think by copying the behavior, they, too, will have fun or be cool.

GENETICS

Researchers have found that some eating disorders, such as anorexia, tend to run in families. There may be genes (segments of DNA, found on chromosomes, that determine the inheritance of particular traits from your mother and father) that can make you more likely to get an eating disorder than someone else. But just because your mother or sister has an eating disorder, doesn't mean that you will definitely have one.

WHAT ARE PERSONAL INFLUENCES?

Eating disorders often begin because of emotional reasons. Low self-esteem and low self-worth are common in people who have eating disorders. So are perfectionism and obsessive-compulsive behaviors. People who have eating disorders try to use food to fill their emotional needs or ease their loneliness.

SELF-IMAGE AND SELF-ESTEEM

Three of the biggest factors in people who have eating disorders are low self-esteem, poor or unrealistic body image, and self-image. The term "body image" refers to how you see your body. "Self-image" is how you think of yourself as a whole, both physically and mentally, including your personality and physical features. "Self-esteem" is how you feel about yourself, your accomplishments, talents, and possibilities. In all three of these areas, how you see yourself may not be how the rest of the world sees you.

Like the crazy mirrors you find at carnivals that distort your image, making you look taller, shorter, wider, or narrower, the mind can play tricks on you and make you believe you look different from the way you really do. It's not unusual for those with eating disorders to have a mildly to

The mind can be very tricky, making you see yourself as heavier, shorter, or taller than you actually are. Low self-esteem can contribute to an eating disorder.

severely distorted view of themselves. And when they compare their body or personality to others, they are very critical of themselves. They look at another person and wish they could be as thin, funny, smart, successful, or happy as that person seems to be. They are also affected, as most of us are, by the images of thin, happy people that are constantly shown in the media. People with eating disorders can't seem to see their own good

27

points because of low self-esteem. They don't value themselves as much as they value those around them.

CHANGES IN BODY IMAGE

At the beginning of the twentieth century, women were thought to be beautiful when they were slightly plump. Seemingly overnight, the image

Body image has changed dramatically in the last one hundred years. This photo, taken in 1925, shows some curvier bodies that were the ideal during the early twentieth century.

of the ideal woman changed completely. Fashion magazines began to show clothing on pencil-thin models, and women all over the world tried to copy that image. But not everyone is meant to be slim or fit any one single image. The desire to match an unrealistic body image can become so great that it triggers an eating disorder.

THE NEED FOR PERFECTION

For those with anorexia or bulimia, not eating is a way of controlling a world they feel is out of control. For binge eaters, eating is a way to avoid dealing with how they feel. They use food to help cope with stress, to take away the pain in their lives, and to give them comfort.

Some people—most commonly athletes, ballet dancers, and models—develop eating disorders because they must maintain a low body weight to be competitive. They may have been encouraged to lose weight by trainers, teachers, or other people who have influence over them. The end result is often disordered eating behaviors.

There's nothing wrong with striving to be the best you can possibly be, but at the same time you need to accept yourself for who you are, with strengths and flaws like any human being. The trouble starts when you lose track of how to balance what you can achieve against what you cannot.

CHAPTER **four**

RECOVERING FROM AN EATING DISORDER

Eating disorders are complex. It takes time, patience, and the help of trained medical professionals to treat them. No single therapy works for all eating disorder patients. A wide variety of treatment plans is needed to help change the way you perceive yourself and find the way to lifelong physical and emotional health. The process could take weeks, months, or even years.

The decision to go forward with recovery is a tough one to make because eating disorders become powerful tools for facing life's pressures and problems. A part of you will want to hold onto that tool for dear life, even when common sense tells you that it may actually end your life.

Part of you doesn't want to give up the eating disorder because it has allowed you to avoid facing the real problems behind it. By focusing on a food obsession and controlling both what you eat and how much you weigh, you've found a way to get around dealing with all those impossibly high expectations and the things in your life you want to control but can't.

HOW TO GET TREATMENT

What happens after you are diagnosed with an eating disorder varies, depending on how severe the disorder is, your physical

Clinical psychologist Angela Redlak counsels a patient at a Charlotte, North Carolina, eating disorder facility. Therapy is an important part of recovery, as is finding the right therapist.

condition, and how involved you are in your own recovery process. To be successful, treatments must address both the physical and psychological aspects of the eating disorder. People with severe eating disorders may require hospitalizations, while others might recover with outpatient therapy. Some people may be helped by medication, while others might do well with a strong nutritional plan.

WHERE TO FIND SUPPORT

Although recovery can only begin when you accept your situation and decide to change, you can't do it alone. Successful recovery takes the understanding and support of everyone around you—especially your family and friends. Just as personal relationships can be among the causes of eating disorders, they also can be an important part of the recovery process.

Finding and confronting the root causes of an eating disorder are difficult and painful processes, and you shouldn't act alone. Medical care and counseling, self-help groups, and your family and friends are all important parts of the recovery process.

HOSPITAL STAYS

The first and most important concern in treating an eating disorder, especially anorexia and bulimia, is to make sure your body is healthy. Dehydration (not having enough liquid in the body), starvation (not having enough nutrients in the body), and electrolyte imbalances (too much or not enough of certain chemicals in the body) can cause serious health problems or even death.

You may be put in a hospital if you:

- Have lost 30 percent of your body weight or more over a period of three months.

While there is no magical cure for an eating disorder, different types of medication have been known to help. A doctor will prescribe the type of medication that is right for you.

- Have a severe metabolic disturbance. This means that your digestive process and the way your body accepts and uses nutrients have been upset. Lack of important nutrients such as potassium, calcium, iron, and others can cause permanent damage to your body in a very short time.
- Have been diagnosed with severe depression or are considered a suicide risk. Staying in a hospital can protect your life until your doctors and therapist help you recover.
- Have been on a binge-and-purge cycle that becomes severe enough to require immediate medical help.
- Have damage to your heart, liver, or kidneys or other medical problems due to long-term starvation from anorexia.

While you're in the hospital, you may get behavioral therapy, family education, group therapy, or medication to help you become better.

TAKING MEDICATION

Medication is often a successful part of eating disorder treatment. No magic pill or potion exists that will relieve eating disorder symptoms or get rid of the disorder altogether, but there are a few medications that can be helpful.

Because depression is a common part of eating disorders, doctors may sometimes prescribe drugs called antidepressants. Antidepressants can be used to help bulimia and binge eating disorder patients recover, especially if they don't respond well to therapy alone. The most common antidepressants used to treat these eating disorders are the selective serotonin reuptake inhibitors (SSRIs). These SSRIs include Prozac, Zoloft, and Paxil. Binge eaters may also benefit from weight-loss drugs such as Xenical. There aren't any drugs that have been shown to help treat anorexia, although behavioral treatments can be effective.

GOING TO THERAPY

Therapy is basically talking to someone—either alone or in a group—who can help you come to terms with the thoughts that led to the eating disorder in order to overcome them. Your therapist can also study other issues that may be involved in your eating disorder, such as depression.

Many treatment programs are based on cognitive behavioral therapy. Cognition is the process of knowing, including perception, memory, and judgment. Cognitive behavioral therapy can help you understand why you developed an eating disorder and learn how to come to terms with the issues that caused it. Several types of therapy are used to treat eating disorders, including the following:

- Individual therapy is when a therapist who is a psychologist, psychiatrist (a psychologist who is also a medical doctor), or social worker works with you one on one.
- Family therapy is geared to help you understand your relationships with your family. Often, family members are involved. Understanding these relationships is important because unresolved issues can complicate your recovery. It is crucial if abuse is at the root of your eating disorder.
- Group therapy is shared therapy sessions with several people who have the same eating disorder. Sharing can help you see that you are not alone in dealing with this problem.

DEVELOPING HEALTHY EATING HABITS

Recovering from an eating disorder means learning healthier eating habits. Eating habits don't change overnight—it takes time and a lot of hard work. Your doctor or counselor may suggest that you keep a food diary so that you remain aware of how, when, where, and what

Part of recovering from an eating disorder includes learning portion control and keeping nutrition in mind while planning meals. Eating can be an enjoyable experience again with the right tools.

you eat. You may meet with a dietician, who can help you plan nutritional meals.

You'll learn about portion control, keeping food stored out of sight, and not going to the grocery store when you're hungry. You'll also learn more positive ways to deal with loneliness, anxiety, and other emotions, and how to reward yourself with things other than food.

Most important, you will learn to listen to your body and trust its innate hunger and fullness signals. This inherent ability to self-regulate what, when, and how much you eat is called intuitive eating.

RECOVER

If you are struggling with an eating disorder, successful recovery depends on one person: you.

MAKING THE COMMITMENT TO GETTING BETTER

Although it takes medical professionals, family, and friends to help you get better, only you can decide to start the recovery process and continue it.

Here are a few things you need to do to truly recover:

- Take part fully in your treatment plan and follow the instructions of your doctor, nutritionist, and therapist. Keep all appointments with your medical and health team, and never lie or hold back information when reporting what you've been doing.
- Be able to function independently in day-to-day living and show that you can cope with any problems or emotional stress that life brings.
- Keep your weight within 5 pounds (2.3 kilograms) of your assigned target weight. If your weight begins to drop (or rise, if you've had problems with bingeing in the past) for any reason, you need to get help right away.

This group of teens who all suffer from eating disorders are practicing a type of therapy called "mindful eating." They eat a "risk food" and then discuss their feelings afterward.

DEVELOPING A GOOD RELATIONSHIP WITH FOOD

Eating disorders are psychological, which means they begin in the mind — in the way we perceive ourselves, our problems, and others around us. Addictions such as drinking and smoking are also psychological disorders. But there's an obvious difference with eating disorders. You can stop smoking, drinking, and taking drugs, but you can't stop eating. You can avoid places where people are smoking, drinking, or using drugs, but it would be tough to avoid places and situations where people eat. So how do people with eating disorders recover when they can never get away from food?

It may sound funny, but you have to make friends with food. You need to learn about hunger, appetite, and satisfaction, and trust your body to know when it's full. And you need to see food as an ally, rather than something that you should avoid, reject, or devour without thought.

RISK OF RELAPSE

Relapse is always a danger with eating disorders. Even with treatment, about 20 percent of people with eating disorders won't recover, according to the organization Anorexia Nervosa and Related Eating Disorders, Inc. That's why anytime there is the slightest hint that you are returning to destructive eating habits, you need to contact your doctor and therapist immediately.

Regardless of the eating disorder, the symptoms of relapse are very similar and may include the following:

- Gaining or losing 5 pounds (2.3 kg) or more from the maintenance weight range
- Increases in addictive behavior, regardless of whether that involves food, exercise, drugs, or alcohol
- A sudden or sharp decrease in appetite or ability to eat
- An episode of purging, along with renewed use of laxatives, diuretics, diet pills, or enemas
- A dramatic change in sleeping patterns—either sleeping more than usual or suddenly being unable to sleep

GETTING HELP FOR A FRIEND

What would you do if you had a good friend who began to show symptoms of an eating disorder?

One approach you could try is talking to your friend about the changes you've noticed. Express your concern for the person's health and happiness. Your friend may become extremely angry with you. Don't be surprised if that happens. It's very hard for someone with an eating disorder to face reality and begin to deal with it. Your friend may not want to change or have others find out about his or her eating problems.

If you do learn that your friend has some type of eating disorder, never promise to help keep it a secret. Even if he or she begs you not to tell, the best thing you can do is talk with someone in authority. That person may be a medical professional, religious leader, teacher, guidance counselor, school nurse, or one of your parents. Whoever you talk to, get help as soon as you can.

Telling someone about your friend's eating disorder may cost you the friendship. But even if that is the case, the alternative is worse because not trying to get help for your friend could endanger his or her health. You cannot make someone with an eating disorder seek help, but you can help that person find help when he or she is ready. Then you can offer your support and be there as your friend recovers.

And if you're hesitant to get involved because you're unsure if the person has an eating disorder, do some research. You'll find a wealth of information from a variety of resources in local libraries, support organizations, and on the Internet. Read up, check up, and follow up if you believe your friend does have an eating disorder.

anorexia nervosa An eating disorder in which a person intention-
ally starves himself or herself.

antidepressant A drug to relieve or prevent depression.

binge To eat large amounts of food in a short period of time, often
in secret and usually without control.

binge eating disorder An eating disorder in which a person eats
large quantities of food all at once on a regular basis.

body image The way in which people see their bodies or their
physical selves.

bulimia nervosa An eating disorder in which people eat normal
or large amounts of food and then rid their bodies of the food by
either forcing themselves to vomit, abusing laxatives or diuretics,
taking enemas, or exercising obsessively.

calorie A unit to measure the energy-producing value of food.

compulsive exercise disorder An eating disorder in which a
person exercises excessively, often for several hours each day, in
order to use any calories that he or she has taken in; also called
exercise addiction.

denial The act of refusing to admit the truth or face the reality of a
situation.

depression A mood disorder in which a person has unusually sad
feelings that last for a long period of time.

deprive To withhold something from or take something away.

disordered eating Attitudes and behaviors toward food and
eating that do not meet the definition of a recognized eating
disorder but still affect a person's mental or physical health.

diuretic A medication that can make you urinate more often. People
with certain types of eating disorders may take diuretics to purge
calories from their bodies.

eating disorder Any problem with food that severely disrupts a person's life.

genetic Relating to how people inherit traits from their parents.

inpatient A patient who remains in a hospital or a clinic for treatment.

internalize To bottle up problems or emotions.

laxative A medication that is normally used to treat constipation but that bulimics and other eating disorder sufferers take in large quantities to purge food from their bodies.

obsessive Excessive to the point of being unreasonable.

outpatient A patient in a clinic or hospital who does not live at the facility but who visits on a regular basis for treatment.

overachiever A person who strives for success beyond what is expected.

psychiatrist A doctor who is trained to treat and counsel people with mental, emotional, or behavioral disorders.

purge To rid the body of food in an unnatural way, usually by vomiting or overusing laxatives.

self-esteem Confidence in or satisfaction with oneself; self-respect.

self-image A person's sense of his or her own body and personality.

therapy Various types of treatment for emotional and psychological problems.

FOR MORE INFORMATION

American Dietetic Association
120 South Riverside Plaza, Suite 2000
Chicago, IL 60606-6995
(800) 877-1600
Web site: http://www.eatright.org
This organization is made up of sixty-five thousand dieticians and
    other eating professionals who are experts in helping people
    make healthier food choices.

Eating Disorders Clinic, Inc.
121 Willowdale Avenue, Suite 205
North York, ON M2N 6A3
Canada
(416) 483-0956
Web site: http://www.eatingdisorders.ca
The Eating Disorders Clinic offers psychotherapy services and sup-
    port for individuals and their families who are affected by eating
    disorders.

gURL
Web site: http://www.gurl.com
This online magazine for young women talks honestly about body
    image.

Jessie's Hope
400-601 West Broadway Street
Vancouver, BC V5Z 4C2
Canada

(604) 689-9854

Web site: http://www.jessieshope.org

Jessie's Hope, a nonprofit organization, provides resources to health professionals, teachers, counselors, and others who work with individuals with eating disorders in an effort to promote positive body image among youth.

National Association of Anorexia Nervosa and Associated Disorders (ANAD)

P.O. Box 7

Highland Park, IL 60035

(847) 831-3438

Web site: http://www.anad.org

ANAD is a resource center that can point you to the best sources and facilities to get treatment.

National Eating Disorders Association (NEDA)

603 Stewart Street, Suite 803

Seattle, WA 98101

(800) 931-2237

Web site: http://www.nationaleatingdisorders.org

NEDA is the largest nonprofit group in the United States working to prevent eating disorders. Contact NEDA, and it will help you find treatment options in your area.

National Institute of Mental Health (NIMH)

6001 Executive Boulevard, Room 8184, MSC 9663

Bethesda, MD 20892-9663

(866) 615-6464

Web site: http://www.nimh.nih.gov
NIMH informs people about all aspects of mental health, including
    eating disorders.

Overeaters Anonymous
P.O. Box 44020
Rio Rancho, NM 87174–4020
(505) 891-2664
Web site: http://www.overeatersanonymous.org
This organization is made up of people who are recovering from
    binge eating.

WEB SITES

Due to the changing nature of Internet links, Rosen Publishing has
developed an online list of Web sites related to the subject of this book.
This site is updated regularly. Please use this link to access the list:

http://www.rosenlinks.com/gh/eat

FOR FURTHER READING

Brown, Harriet. *Brave Girl Eating: A Family's Struggle with Anorexia*. New York, NY: HarperCollins, 2010.

Challem, Jack. *The Food-Mood Solution: All-Natural Ways to Banish Anxiety, Depression, Anger, Stress, Overeating, and Alcohol and Drug Problems—and Feel Good Again*. Indianapolis, IN: Wiley, 2008.

Costin, Carolyn. *The Eating Disorder Sourcebook*. New York, NY: McGraw-Hill, 2006.

Craighead, Linda W. *The Appetite Awareness Workbook: How to Listen to Your Body and Overcome Bingeing, Overeating, & Obsession with Food*. Oakland, CA: New Harbinger, 2006.

Hornbacher, Marya. *Wasted: A Memoir of Anorexia and Bulimia*. New York, NY: Harper Perennial, 2006.

Kessler, David, M.D. *The End of Overeating: Taking Control of the Insatiable American Appetite*. Emmaus, PA: Rodale, 2010.

Lawton, Sandra Augustyn. *Eating Disorders Information for Teens: Health Tips About Anorexia, Bulimia, Binge Eating, and Other Eating Disorders*. Detroit, MI: Omnigraphics, 2005.

Phillips, Katherine A., M.D. *The Broken Mirror: Understanding and Treating Body Dysmorphic Disorder*. Revised and expanded ed. New York, NY: Oxford University Press, 2005.

Ross, Carolyn. *The Binge Eating & Compulsive Overeating Workbook: An Integrated Approach to Overcoming Disordered Eating*. Oakland, CA: New Harbinger, 2009.

Schaefer, Jenni. *Goodbye Ed, Hello Me: Recover from Your Eating Disorder and Fall in Love with Life*. New York, NY: McGraw-Hill, 2009.

Schlosser, Eric. *Chew on This: Everything You Don't Want to Know About Fast Food*. Boston, MA: Houghton Mifflin, 2006.

ABOUT THE AUTHORS

Tammy Laser writes books for teens and lives in New York City.

Stephanie Watson is an author and editor and lives in Atlanta, Georgia.

PHOTO CREDITS

Cover, p. 1 © www.istockphoto.com/Aldo Murillo; p. 5 Hemera/Thinkstock; p. 7 Jamie Grill/Iconica/Getty Images; p. 9 © www.istockphoto.com/Dr. Heinz Linke; p. 13 © Maxppp/ZUMA Press; p. 16 © Bubbles Photolibrary/Alamy; p. 20 © www.istockphoto.com/Chris Bernard; p. 24 Don Arnold/WireImage/Getty Images; p. 27 Ana Abejon/Vetta/Getty Images; p. 28 Topical Press Agency/Hulton Archive/Getty Images; p. 31 © Gary O'Brien/MCT/Landov; p. 33 SW Productions/Photodisc/Getty Images; p. 36 © www.istockphoto.com/Anthony Ladd; p. 38 krtphotoslive/Newscom.

Designer: Nicole Russo; Editor: Bethany Bryan;
Photo Researcher: Amy Feinberg